DO
THINGS
THAT MATTER
TO
YOUR HEART

Caroline, 71 years old

What advice would your 80-year-old
self give you?

That's the question artist Susan
O'Malley asked ordinary people of
all ages. She then transformed their
responses into vibrant text-based
images, collected in *Advice from My
80-Year-Old Self* (Chronicle Books).

ISBN 978-1-4521-5487-9

Manufactured in China

MIX
Paper from
responsible sources
FSC™ C020056

Design by Brooke Johnson

From *Do Things That Matter to Your
Heart Notebook Collection* published
in 2017 by Chronicle Books LLC.

CHRONICLE BOOKS
680 SECOND STREET
SAN FRANCISCO, CA 94107
WWW.CHRONICLEBOOKS.COM

ART
BEFORE
DISHES

Lea, 62 years old

What advice would your 80-year-old
self give you?

That's the question artist Susan
O'Malley asked ordinary people of
all ages. She then transformed their
responses into vibrant text-based
images, collected in *Advice from My
80-Year-Old Self* (Chronicle Books).

ISBN 978-1-4521-5487-9

Manufactured in China

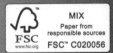

MIX
Paper from
responsible sources
FSC™ C020056

Design by Brooke Johnson

From *Do Things That Matter to Your
Heart Notebook Collection* published
in 2017 by Chronicle Books LLC.

CHRONICLE BOOKS
680 SECOND STREET
SAN FRANCISCO, CA 94107
WWW.CHRONICLEBOOKS.COM

LESS
INTERNET
MORE
LOVE

Kelly, 25 years old

What advice would your 80-year-old
self give you?

That's the question artist Susan
O'Malley asked ordinary people of
all ages. She then transformed their
responses into vibrant text-based
images, collected in *Advice from My
80-Year-Old Self* (Chronicle Books).

ISBN 978-1-4521-5487-9

Manufactured in China

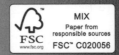

MIX
Paper from
responsible sources
FSC™ C020056

FSC
www.fsc.org

Design by Brooke Johnson

From *Do Things That Matter to Your
Heart Notebook Collection* published
in 2017 by Chronicle Books LLC.

CHRONICLE BOOKS
680 SECOND STREET
SAN FRANCISCO, CA 94107
WWW.CHRONICLEBOOKS.COM